GOSCINNY AND UDERZO

PRESENT

An Asterix Adventure

ASTERIX
AND THE ACTRESS

Written and Illustrated by ALBERT UDERZO

Translated by ANTHEA BELL *and* DEREK HOCKRIDGE

*à Hugo
mon petit-fils*

Original title: *Astérix et Latraviata*

Original edition © 2001 Les Éditions Albert René/ Goscinny-Uderzo
English translation: © 2001 Les Éditions Albert René/ Goscinny-Uderzo

Exclusive licensee: Orion Publishing Group
Translators: Anthea Bell and Derek Hockridge
Lettering and text layout: Bryony Newhouse
Inking: Fréderic Mébarki
Colour work: Thierry Mébarki
Co-ordination: Studio 'Et Cetera'

Hardback edition first published in Great Britain in 2001
by Orion Books Ltd

This edition first published in Great Britain in 2002 by
Orion Books Ltd
Orion House, 5 Upper St Martin's Lane
London WC2H 9EA

Printed in Italy
www.asterix.tm.fr

A CIP catalogue record for this book
is available from the British Library

ISBN 0 75284 658 2

Distributed in the United States of America by
Sterling Publishing Co., Inc.
387 Park Avenue South, New York,
NY 10016-8810

GAULISH VILLAGE

COMPENDIUM

LAUDANUM

AQUARIUM

TOTORUM

ARMORICA

BELGICA

LUTETIA

GAUL
(ROMAN CONQUEST)
50 BC

CELTICA

AQUITANIA

PROVINCIA

THE YEAR IS 50 BC. GAUL IS ENTIRELY OCCUPIED BY THE
ROMANS. WELL, NOT ENTIRELY...ONE SMALL VILLAGE OF
THE INDOMITABLE GAULS STILL HOLDS OUT AGAINST THE
INVADERS. AND LIFE IS NOT EASY FOR THE ROMAN LEGION-
ARIES WHO GARRISON THE FORTIFIED CAMPS OF TOTORUM,
AQUARIUM, LAUDANUM AND COMPENDIUM...

ASTERIX, THE HERO OF THESE ADVENTURES. A SHREWD, CUNNING LITTLE WARRIOR, ALL PERILOUS MISSIONS ARE IMMEDIATELY ENTRUSTED TO HIM. ASTERIX GETS HIS SUPERHUMAN STRENGTH FROM THE MAGIC POTION BREWED BY THE DRUID GETAFIX . . .

OBELIX, ASTERIX'S INSEPARABLE FRIEND. A MENHIR DELIVERY-MAN BY TRADE, ADDICTED TO WILD BOAR. OBELIX IS ALWAYS READY TO DROP EVERYTHING AND GO OFF ON A NEW ADVENTURE WITH ASTERIX – SO LONG AS THERE'S WILD BOAR TO EAT, AND PLENTY OF FIGHTING. HIS CONSTANT COMPANION IS DOGMATIX, THE ONLY KNOWN CANINE ECOLOGIST, WHO HOWLS WITH DESPAIR WHEN A TREE IS CUT DOWN.

GETAFIX, THE VENERABLE VILLAGE DRUID, GATHERS MISTLETOE AND BREWS MAGIC POTIONS. HIS SPECIALITY IS THE POTION WHICH GIVES THE DRINKER SUPERHUMAN STRENGTH. BUT GETAFIX ALSO HAS OTHER RECIPES UP HIS SLEEVE . . .

CACOFONIX, THE BARD. OPINION IS DIVIDED AS TO HIS MUSICAL GIFTS. CACOFONIX THINKS HE'S A GENIUS. EVERY-ONE ELSE THINKS HE'S UNSPEAKABLE. BUT SO LONG AS HE DOESN'T SPEAK, LET ALONE SING, EVERYBODY LIKES HIM . . .

FINALLY, VITALSTATISTIX, THE CHIEF OF THE TRIBE. MAJESTIC, BRAVE AND HOT-TEMPERED, THE OLD WARRIOR IS RESPECTED BY HIS MEN AND FEARED BY HIS ENEMIES. VITALSTATISTIX HIMSELF HAS ONLY ONE FEAR, HE IS AFRAID THE SKY MAY FALL ON HIS HEAD TOMORROW. BUT AS HE ALWAYS SAYS, TOMORROW NEVER COMES.

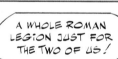

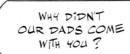

OH, AND YOUR DAD SAYS HE'S SORRY HE CAN'T BE WITH US, AND HE'S SENT YOU THIS SWORD AS A PRESENT!

!?

JUST WHAT I WANTED! JUDGING BY THE PRECIOUS STONES ON ITS SHEATH, IT MUST HAVE BELONGED TO SOME RICH ROMAN OFFICER!

ACTUALLY IT BELONGED TO A DRUNK... A FORMER LEGIONARY. HE SWAPPED IT WITH US FOR A BARREL OF BARLEY BEER!

SMACK!

SCRUNCH! SCRUNCH!

HE LEFT US THIS HELMET TOO. YOU CAN ADD IT TO YOUR COLLECTION, OBELIXIWIXIKINS!

!

PFFFFF

ANYBODY WANT TO TRY THIS HELMET ON? IF SO I'M READY TO JAM IT ON HIS HEAD, HARD! THAT'LL TEACH HIM TO TRY THINGS ON WITH ME!

4A

MEANWHILE, IN CONDATUM...

MODERNITIES & COLLECTABLES

GAULISH POTTERY IS AN EXCELLENT INVESTMENT, BOUND TO APPRECIATE IN VALUE. IT'S GOT A GREAT FUTURE AHEAD OF IT!

WE HAVE MENHIRS IN ALL SIZES AVAILABLE, HAND-CRAFTED, SIGNED, CARVED FROM PURE ARMORICAN GRANITE!

OBELIX

ROLL UP, FOLKS, ROLL UP! WHO DOESN'T HAVE A DOLMEN YET? EASY SELF-ASSEMBLY!

UNUSED HELMET

SLIGHTLY USED HELMET

4B

11

LATER, IN THE VILLAGE...

RIGHT! VANILLA AND I HAVE DECIDED TO HAVE A REAL BIRTHDAY PARTY FOR YOU TWO!

BUT...

...BUT WE'VE ALREADY HAD A BIRTHDAY BANQUET FOR THE WHOLE VILLAGE!

IF YOU ASK ME, THAT WAS JUST AN EXCUSE FOR THE USUAL BINGE!

I LIKE A BINGE EVEN WHEN IT ISN'T MY BIRTHDAY!

WELL THIS TIME WE'RE GOING TO INVITE ALL THE BARDS FROM THE SURROUNDING VILLAGES TO PLAY MUSIC SO THAT THE YOUNG PEOPLE OF OUR OWN VILLAGE CAN DANCE!

INCLUDING YOU TWO, OF COURSE!

MEANWHILE, YOU CAN MAKE YOURSELVES USEFUL...

...BY PICKING SOME PRETTY FLOWERS TO DECORATE THE VILLAGE!

10A

I STILL SAY THERE'S NOTHING I LIKE BETTER THAN A BANQUET ON MY BIRTHDAY!

YES, AND I BET I KNOW TWO PEOPLE ENJOYING PLENTY OF BANQUETS!!!

Fishmonger UNHYGIEN

BY BELENOS! WHAT ARE OUR BOYS WAITING FOR? WHY DON'T THEY COME TO THE RESCUE?

THEY'D HAVE TO KNOW WHERE WE ARE FIRST!

WELL, BOGUS GENIUS, SO WHAT'S THIS SOLUTION OF YOURS?

?

HERE IT IS!!

10B

14

AND JUST HOW DOES THIS GAULISH WOMAN THINK SHE CAN RECOVER MY WEAPONS?

ONE OF THE GAULS IN THE VILLAGE HOLDING YOUR PROPERTY IS VERY SUSCEPTIBLE TO THE CHARMS OF A GAULISH GIRL CALLED PANACEA!

AND NOW, STRAIGHT FROM THE ROMAN THEATRE, LET ME PRESENT THE GREAT TRAGIC ACTRESS LATRAVIATA! A LITTLE CLEVER MAKE-UP HAS TURNED HER INTO A PERFECT REPLICA OF THIS PANACEA! HER CHARM AND ACTING ABILITY, WILL DO THE REST!

BUT SUPPOSE THE REAL PANACEA TURNS UP IN THE VILLAGE?

NEVER FEAR! THE REAL PANACEA LIVES HERE IN CONDATUM WITH HER HUSBAND!

BUT SUPPOSE LATRAVIATA'S CHARM DOESN'T WORK?

AND SUPPOSE THIS POMPOUS IDIOT POMPEY STOPS ASKING STUPID QUESTIONS?

11A

LOOK AT THOSE TWO GREAT GOOFS! CAN'T EVEN SUMMON UP THE COURAGE TO ASK A GIRL TO DANCE!

AFTER WE WENT TO ALL THAT TROUBLE, TOO!

11B

I HAVE A NASTY FEELING WE'RE GOING TO END OUR DAYS HERE IN JUG, OBELISCOIDIX!

AND I BET EVERYONE THINKS WE'RE OUT ON THE TILES WITH A BARREL OF BARLEY BEER!

SHUT UP ABOUT JUGS AND BAR-RELS, WILL YOU!

DON'T YOU WORRY, YOU OLD SOAK! IN HIS CLEMENCY, THE PREFECT HAS DECIDED TO SET YOU FREE TOMORROW!

OH! THANK YOU! THE BLESSINGS OF BACCHUS ON THE MAGNANIMOUS BOGUS GENIUS! MAY HIS CUP ALWAYS RUN OVER!

YOU'RE GET-TING OFF LIGHTLY, TREMENSDELIRIUS...

...YOU'VE ONLY GOT TO DO TWO PUNISHMENT FATIGUES STOCKING UP THE WATER SUPPLY!

MERCY! NO! NOT THAT! I CAN'T STAND CONTACT WITH WATER!!!

SO WE GUESSED!

THOSE BLIGHTERS WANT TO POISON ME!

WE HAVE A PROPOSITION TO PUT TO YOU, ROMAN!

WE GUESS YOU'LL BE ABLE TO LEAVE THE PREFECTURE BETWEEN YOUR TWO PUNISHMENT FATIGUES, RIGHT?

YEAH ... SO WHAT?

THIS PURSE FULL OF SESTERTII IS YOURS IF YOU PROMISE TO TELL OUR FRIENDS PANACEA AND TRAGICOMIX WHERE WE ARE! THEY LIVE IN THIS CITY!

YES, YES! I'LL DO IT! PANACEA AND TRAGI-COMIX! IT'S A DEAL!

SOMEONE OUGHT TO GO AND SEE TRAGICOMIX IN CONDATUM! IT COULD BE URGENT!

OBELIX AND I WILL GO, GETA-FIX! WE CAN CALL AND SEE OUR FATHERS TOO!

SUPPOSE I WAS TO SING JUST A TEENY-TINY POETIC ODE TO PANACEA

ASTERIX! **HAVE YOU BEEN DRINKING?!**

WOO-ER!

OH NO!

AREN'T YOU ASHAMED OF YOURSELF? IF YOUR FATHER COULD SEE YOU NOW!!

WOO-ER!

SEE YOU LATER, THEN, ASTERIX!

PSSST! HOW'S IT GOING?

NO LUCK THIS TIME, BUT I'M NOT BEATEN YET!

I'M SURE IT WAS THAT LITTLE MADAM'S FAULT YOU WERE DRINKING!!

GLUG... WOO-ER!

WHATEVER I DO I CAN'T GET HIM BACK TO NORMAL! I'LL GO AND ASK VANILLA TO HELP ME!

20A

I'M WORRIED, VANILLA! ASTERIX HAS COME HOME WITH PANACEA IN A VERY STRANGE STATE!

MY LAD'S IN A STRANGE STATE TOO! HE WON'T FINISH UP HIS NICE SOUP, EVEN GARNISHED WITH ROAST BOAR!

THAT PANACEA IS BAD NEWS FOR OUR BOYS!

YES. I THINK WE'D BETTER CONSULT THE DRUID GETAFIX. HIS WISDOM WILL COME TO OUR AID!

PSST! IT'S ALL RIGHT, THE COAST IS CLEAR!

WHERE ARE YOU GOING THIS TIME PANACEA?!

DON'T WORRY, SOPORIF... I MEAN DAD!

THE MORE I SEE OF MY DAUGHTER, THE LESS LIKE HERSELF SHE SEEMS!

20B

24

25

SOME GREAT EMOTIONAL SHOCK MUST HAVE LEFT HIM IN THIS STATE!

WOO-ER!

BUT EMOTIONAL OR NOT, HE CERTAINLY NEEDS HELP!

GLUP! WOO-ER! GLUP!

YAHOOOOoo!

22A

YIPPEEE!

POC!

COME BACK HERE THIS MINUTE, ASTERIX!

YiPPEE

FULLIAVTOMATIX

UNHYGIENX

20B

OH, WONDERFUL STUFF, YOUR POTION! NOW MY SON THINKS HE'S A GIANT FLEA!!!

I HAVE TO CONFESS I DIDN'T FORESEE THESE SPECIAL EFFECTS.

WELL, DO SOMETHING, DON'T JUST STAND THERE TWIDDLING YOUR THUMBS!!!

LISTEN, SARSAPARILLA! I MAY HAVE INVENTED A POTION WHICH GIVES PEOPLE SUPERHUMAN STRENGTH, AND ANOTHER WHICH TURNS THEM INTO GRANITE AND MAKES THEM REVERT TO CHILDHOOD, BUT DO YOU EXPECT ME TO WORK MIRACLES?

YOU SEE, DOG-MATIX, WITHOUT ASTERIX I FEEL AS IF THE STUFFING WAS KNOCKED OUT OF ME!

BONG!

WHOOMPH!

22C

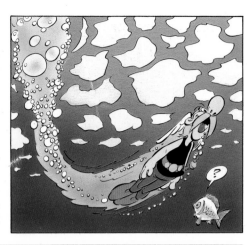

WE'RE A LONG WAY FROM THE COAST WHERE THAT CANTANKEROUS LITTLE GAUL LIVES, BUT WE'D BETTER BE CAREFUL ALL THE SAME!

CETERARUM RERUM PRUDENS!

I SEE A SHIP OVER THERE! I'M SAVED!

AHOY! AHOY THERE!

THE GAU... THE GAUGAU...

CRAASH!

WHAT DO YOU MEAN, THE GAULS? WHAT DO YOU MEAN, THE GAULS? I DON'T SEE ANY GAULS, DO YOU?

SO WHAT DO YOU THINK THAT IS, THEN ???

IT'S A GHOST!

I SPY A SPOOK!

BEAR HARD TO STARBOARD!!!

I'M GOING ASHORE FOR PSYCHOANALYSIS!

?!

SPECTRAL ANALYSIS MIGHT DO THE TRICK, CAP'N!

32

IN CONDATUM, WHERE NIGHT HAS FALLEN...

WOW, DID I EVER HAVE A THIRSHT ON ME... HIC, HAEC, HOC!... BACK IN THE PREFECT'S PRISHON!

FACT IS, THEY WEREN'T PLEASHED I DID A DEAL WITH POMPEY'S SHWORD AND ... HIC! ... HELMET ... BOTTOMSH UP! HEE, HEE, HEE!

IT'S LATE, TIME FOR BED, TREMENSDELIRIUS!

POMPEY ISN'T PLEASHED EITHER... HIC! ...HE'S AFRAID CAESHAR WILL FIND OUT HE'SH IN GAUL ... HIC! ...TO RAISHE AN ARMY AGAINSHT HIM... HIC! TEEHEEHEE...

I SHEEM TO REMEMBER I WAS SHUPPOSHED TO WARN SHOMEONE... HIC!... CAN'T RE-MEMBER WHO ... HIC! ... 'BOUT CAN'T REMEMBER WHAT! HIC!

SNORRR! ZZZZZ!

29A

A LITTLE LATER, AT THE HEADQUARTERS OF THE LEGATE COMMANDING THE REGION...

WHAT?

LEGATORIA PROVINCIA

QUICK! I WANT A MESSENGER SENT TO CAESAR IN ROME!

AND ONCE AGAIN WE HAVE A PRIVILEGED VIEW OF...

...THE MAGNIFICENT ORGANISATION OF THE ROMAN ARMY...

...EVEN IF SOMETIMES...

JUST LET ME GET MY HANDS ON THE SON OF A ✱◉✿∿ WHO STOLE MY HORSE...

29B

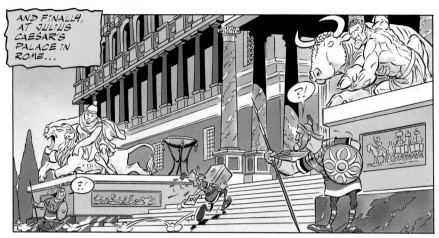

AND FINALLY, AT JULIUS CAESAR'S PALACE IN ROME...

?!

?!

AN URGENT MESSAGE FOR CAESAR!

ARRRRRRG! WHEEEEZE! ARRRRRRG! WHEEZE!

BY JUPITER! POMPEY!!! NOT HIM AGAIN?

AN URGENT MESSAGE FOR THE LEGATE IN CONDATUM!

AND YET AGAIN WE CAN ADMIRE THE EFFICIENCY OF THE ROMAN POSTAL SERVICE IN ACTION, IN THE OTHER DIRECTION.

THEY SAY THEY'RE GOING TO STOP THE PRICE OF A NEW HORSE FROM MY PAY! TALK ABOUT A RUN OF BAD LUCK!

ROMA

THE LAST RUNNER FINALLY RELAYS CAESAR'S MESSAGE TO THE LEGATE IN CONDATUM.

ARRRRRRG! WHEEEEZE! ARRRRRRG! WHEEEEZE!

KNOCK KNOCK KNOCK KNOCK

GENTLEMEN, YOU WILL NOW BE AWARE THAT POMPEY IS HERE IN GAUL TO RAISE AN ARMY AGAINST CAESAR, WHO ORDERS US TO INVESTIGATE ALL THE GARRISONS AND FIND THE TRAITORS! SO GET MOVING!

MEANWHILE, STILL IN CONDATUM...

I THINK I'LL CALL ON ASTERIX AND OBELIX'S PARENTS. IT'S A LONG TIME SINCE I LAST SAW THEM!

FOR THIS IS THE REAL PANACEA!

?!

MODERNITY

THE PREFECT'S GUARDS TOOK ASTRONOMIX AND OBELISCOÏDIX AWAY! I NEVER SAW THEM AGAIN!

?!

OH, TRAGICOMIX!! ASTRONOMIX AND OBELISCOÏDIX ARE IN DANGER!

WE MUST GO TO THE VILLAGE AT ONCE AND WARN ASTERIX AND OBELIX!

CLAC!

AT THIS VERY MOMENT, IN THE VILLAGE...

I FINALLY MANAGED TO MAKE OFF WITH THE SWORD WHILE ASTERIX AND HIS MOTHER WERE OUT!

THEN LET'S GET OUT OF HERE, QUICK!

WE WANT TO ASK YOU A FAVOUR, ROMAN!

GULP!

31 A

WE HAVE TO GO TO CONDATUM! WOULD YOU LEND US YOUR CART? IT WOULD GET US THERE FASTER!

ER...WELL... THE FACT IS...

I WAS JUST ASKING FASTANDFURIUS TO TAKE ME BACK TO CONDATUM MYSELF! WE CAN TRAVEL TOGETHER!

I'LL HARNESS UP THE HORSES!

I'M GLAD TO HEAR YOU'VE CHANGED YOUR MIND, PANACEA!

BUT NOT SO LONG AGO SHE WAS SAYING...

LA DONNA È MOBILE, OBELIX!

LATER, ON THE WAY TO CONDATUM...

DID YOU REALLY HAVE TO LUMBER US WITH A MENHIR?

SO? I CAN GIVE MY DAD A PRESENT IF I WANT TO, RIGHT?

YOU DON'T SEEM QUITE YOURSELF, OBELIX, OLD FRIEND!

I'M SAD! I'VE LOST MY LITTLE DOGMATIX!

31 B

IN ONE OF THE MANY ROMAN GARRISONS ON OCCUPIED ARMORICAN SOIL...

CENTURION GYMNASTICAPPARATUS, YOUR ORDERS ARE TO INVESTIGATE THE WHOLE SECTOR IN ORDER TO IDENTIFY AND EXPOSE THE LEGIONS IN POMPEY'S PAY!

IT WON'T BE EASY IF THEY DON'T HAVE ANY DISTINGUISHING MARKS, GENERAL!

NEVER MIND THAT! GET MOVING!!!

?!

DECURION COUGHLINCTUS! YOU AND YOUR MEN ARE TO COMB THE WHOLE SECTOR AND PICK UP POMPEIANS, WHO ARE LEGION HERE!

JUST AS YOU SAY, CENTURION, BUT 'SCUSE ME ASKING, HOW DO I RECOGNISE A POMPARIAN WHEN I SEE ONE?

NEVER MIND THAT! GET MOVING!!!

POP!

GOT IT, YOU BUNCH OF SKIVERS? WE COMB THE SECTOR, WE PICK UP ALL THE POMPARIANS WE FIND, AND WE REPORT BACK. ANY QUESTIONS?

NEVER MIND THAT! GET MOVING!!!

?! ?! ?! ?! ?! ?! ?! ?!

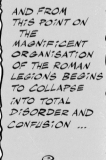

AND FROM THIS POINT ON THE MAGNIFICENT ORGANISATION OF THE ROMAN LEGIONS BEGINS TO COLLAPSE INTO TOTAL DISORDER AND CONFUSION...

HALT! WHO GOES THERE? ARE YOU THE POMPARIAN LEGIONARIES WE'RE AFTER? IF SO, IT'S A FAIR COP!

YOU'LL BE COPPING IT YOURSELF IF YOU DON'T WATCH OUT!

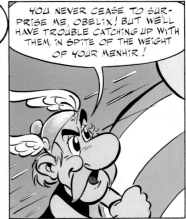

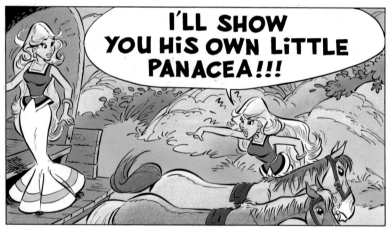

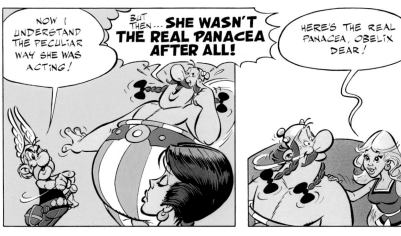

WE MUST GO TO CONDATUM, OBELIX, AND FAST!

?!

WOO-ER!

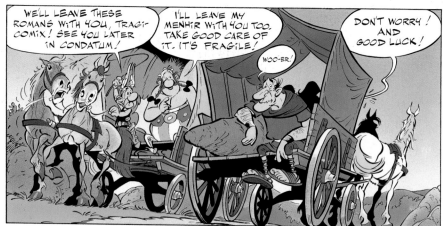

WE'LL LEAVE THESE ROMANS WITH YOU, TRAGI-COMIX! SEE YOU LATER IN CONDATUM!

I'LL LEAVE MY MENHIR WITH YOU TOO. TAKE GOOD CARE OF IT. IT'S FRAGILE!

DON'T WORRY! AND GOOD LUCK!

WOO-ER!

AND WHILE WE THOUGHT OUR DADS WERE LIVING IT UP, THEY WERE ON DRY BREAD AND WATER!

TELL ME, ASTERIX, WHAT IS ALL THIS ABOUT THE SWORD AND HELMET AND A POMPOUS PREFECT AND CAESAR?

WELL, ONCE UPON A TIME ROME WAS GOVERNED BY A *TRIUMVIRATE* ... THAT MEANS THREE CONSULS: *CAESAR*, *POMPEY* AND *CRASSUS*. WHEN *CRASSUS* DIED CAESAR DISMISSED POMPEY IN ORDER TO MAKE HIMSELF DICTATOR, SO THAT MADE *POMPEY* HIS GREATEST ENEMY. I CAN WELL IMAGINE THAT HE'S TRYING TO RAISE AN ARMY AGAINST CAESAR IN GAUL, WHICH WOULD EXPLAIN A CERTAIN AMOUNT OF CONFUSION AMONG THE ROMAN LEGIONS. UNDERSTAND?

NO!....

BUT I DO UNDERSTAND ONE THING... **THESE ROMANS ARE CRAZY!**

TAP! TAP! TAP!

38A

OH, LET THE ROMANS SETTLE THEIR OWN DIFFERENCES! IT'S NONE OF OUR BUSINESS, OBELIX!

ALL THE SAME... WHAT A WASTE!

PAF! BONG! THUD! PIF!

CONDATE

38B

42

ONLY PASSING THROUGH!

ASTERIX, OBELIX! AT LAST!!!

DAD!

I FELT I WAS GROWING OLD DOWN HERE, SON!

MY BABY BOY! IT'S GOOD TO SEE YOU!!

AND HOW'S YOUR MOTHER?

SHE'S JUST FINE, EXCEPT HER ONE IDEA IS TO MARRY ME OFF!

ANY NEWS APART FROM THAT?

!

WELL, BOGUS GENIUS? A RAT LEAVING THE SINKING SHIP?

WELL, PREFECT? LEAVING US WITHOUT SAYING GOODBYE?!

WE TOLD YOU TO WAIT FOR OUR SONS TO TURN UP!

!

STOP THAT TRAITOR!

THOSE ARE THE TRAITORS! THEY'VE GOT POMPEY'S WEAPONS!

I THINK WE'LL HAVE TO BE VERY VERY POLITE TO THEM AGAIN, OBELIX!

YOU KNOW WHAT? I SHALL NEVER REGRET VISITING CONDATUM!

I KNOW, BUT ALL THE SAME, CAN YOU TELL ME IF YOU HAPPEN TO HAVE SEEN POMPEY AND THAT TRAITOR BOGUS GENIUS?

YES, OF COURSE!

I MET BOGUS GENIUS A MOMENT AGO, AND HE'S JUST MET RATHER A LOT OF LEGIONARIES HIMSELF. AS FOR POMPEY...

WOULD THIS BE THE MAN YOU'RE AFTER, CAESAR?

HE RAN INTO ME JUST NOW. HE SEEMED TO BE IN A HURRY TO LEAVE CONDATUM!

SINCE IT'S A CHANGE OF AIR THEY'RE AFTER, I'LL HAVE THEM SHIPPED OFF TO THE DESERTS OF AFRICA. THAT'LL COOL THEM DOWN A BIT!

42ᴬ

AND LET IT NEVER BE SAID THAT CAESAR WAS UNGRATEFUL! GAULS, YOU DESERVE THE TROPHY I AM GOING TO GIVE YOU!

IT'S A **GOLDEN ME!**

WHAT'S A GOLDEN MEAN?

HE SAID A GOLDEN ME ... PROBABLY A GOLDEN STATUE OF HIMSELF!

THANKS, JULES, BUT THE PERSON WHO REALLY DESERVES A TROPHY ...

?!?

...IS THE GREAT ACTRESS LATRAVIATA, WHO HAS GIVEN US A DEMONSTRATION OF HER HISTRIONIC GENIUS!

GIVE A WOMAN A TROPHY FOR ACTING? THAT'S RIDICULOUS!

42ᴮ

LATER... WE'LL HAVE OUR WORK CUT OUT, GETTING THIS PLACE STRAIGHT AGAIN!

OH, MANY HANDS MAKE LIGHT WORK!

I MUST ASK YOU TO FORGIVE ME FOR MY PART IN ALL THIS...

WE BEAR NO GRUDGES...

AND WE'RE GOING TO GIVE YOU...

?!

...SOMETHING...

...WHICH WILL SUIT YOU DOWN TO THE GROUND!

A ROMAN LADY LEFT THIS ROBE WITH US. SHE LOST EVERYTHING BUT HER SANDALS AT DICE!

AND A LITTLE LATER STILL...

CLAP! CLAP! CLAP! CLAP! CLAP! CLAP! CLAP!

I SHALL NEVER FORGET THE GENEROSITY OF THOSE SO UNJUSTLY DESCRIBED AS BARBARIANS!

AND NOW I MUST LEAVE YOU. I'M GETTING FASTAND-FURIUS TO TAKE ME BACK TO ROME.

WOO-ER!

HE LOOKS STONED OUT OF HIS MIND! ONE OF YOUR MENHIRS, WAS IT?

WELL, ONLY A LITTLE ONE!

GOODBYE, ASTERIX! THANKS TO YOU, THIS GOLDEN TROPHY WILL OPEN THE DOORS OF EVERY THEATRE IN ROME TO ME!

OH, IT WAS NOTHING!

SMACK!

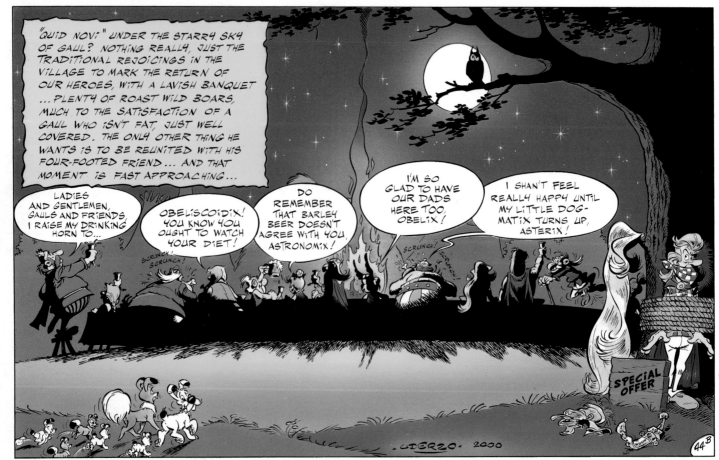